Series editor: Alan White

# HITLER AND THE ROAD TO WAR

## Ted Townley

600050810

Collins Educational

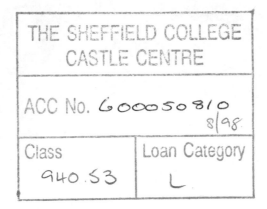
Published by Collins Educational
An imprint of HarperCollins*Publishers* Ltd
77–85 Fulham Palace Road
London W6 8JB

© HarperCollins*Publishers* Ltd 1998

First published 1998

ISBN 0 00 327118 8

Ted Townley asserts the moral right to be
identified as the author of this work.

**British Library Cataloguing in
Publication Data**
A catalogue record for this book is available
from the British Library.

**Acknowledgements**

The author wishes to thank Dr G. Douds and
Dr P. McNally of Worcester College of Higher
Education for their help in the production of
this book, and also the library staff of the
College for their invariable courtesy and
kindness.

The author and publishers would like to thank
the following for permission to reproduce
illustrations:

Centre for Cartoons & Caricature, University
of Kent (p20), Solo Syndication (p25),
Topham Picturepoint (p27).

**Cover photograph**: Photo montage by
John Heartfield, David King Collection.

Edited by Lucy Courtenay
Series design by Derek Lee
Maps drawn by Raymond Turvey
Picture research by Lucy Courtenay
Production by Sue Cashin

Printed and bound by Scotprint Ltd,
Musselburgh

# Contents

# 1 Introduction

*The issues for historians*

## Explanations for the origins of the Second World War

Early explanations largely or entirely assumed that the outbreak of the war could be explained in terms of Hitler's relentless nationalist ambitions, central to Nazi ideology, which led to careful plans for European domination.

A reappraisal came in the 1960s, when Hitler was presented as a supreme opportunist in foreign affairs who took advantage of situations rather than planned them. But in August 1939, he made a fatal miscalculation about the likely reactions of Britain and France to his attack on Poland, which plunged Europe into war.

A linked issue has been how far German expansionism after 1933 can be attributed to Hitler and the Nazis alone, and how far it should be seen as arising from German history since the unification of the country in 1871. The issue of German history was especially related to the ambitions of Germany's rulers prior to the 1914–18 war.

The economic motives behind expansionism have also been stressed. Germany was seen as facing a crisis with regard to food and raw materials (particularly oil and iron ore imports) in the late 1930s. This crisis, it is argued, drove Germany to territorial expansion eastwards.

Explanations of the origins of the war must also embrace the roles of European powers other than Germany. From the start of the debate among historians, the roles of Britain, France and the Soviet Union have been seen as central.

The outbreak of war in September 1939 can no longer be explained simply in terms of Hitler's actions and policies. These nevertheless continue to provide a useful avenue of analysis for those studying the origins of the Second World War, and they provide the framework for the next four chapters of this book. Wider issues are then returned to in the concluding two chapters.

# 2  The origins of Hitler's foreign policy

*What did Hitler's foreign policy owe to German history, and what to Nazi ideology?*

---

## Key points

◆ The German legacy from the First World War
◆ Nazi foreign policy commitments in 1933
◆ International relations before 1933
◆ The international economic crisis after 1929

---

## The German legacy from the First World War

Unification in 1871 gave Germany the potential to upset the balance of power across both Eastern and Western Europe. In 1914 in Berlin, there had been a willingness to chance military conflict in order to break the perceived Franco-Russian encirclement of Germany. This led to rash open promises of support being given to Austria-Hungary. Kaiser Wilhelm II, the Chancellor Bethmann Hollweg, and the German military leaders Hindenburg, Ludendorff and Admiral Tirpitz were at one on this.

The collapse of Russia in 1917 extended the scope of this policy. Germany came close to achieving total domination of Eastern Europe in the Treaty of Brest–Litovsk, when the Russians had to surrender all of Poland and Lithuania to Germany. These gains were welcomed with wild enthusiasm in German right-wing circles and by the army, which saw the new lands as a source of food supplies for the war in Western Europe. The fruits of the treaty were snatched away in 1918, when German forces were defeated on the Western Front.

Thanks to the collapse of the Russian and Austrian empires, the Paris Peace Conference still left Germany in a potentially strong position in Europe, despite all its territorial and other losses. However, before Germany could take advantage of this, the shackles of financial penalties and military restrictions imposed by the Allies at Versailles would have to be broken.

The severity of the Versailles terms imposed on Germany in 1919 made it more likely that Germans would insist on their reversal. Even democratic politicians of the 1920s like Stresemann could not accept the loss of German lands in the east to the new state of Poland, which now divided the German province of East Prussia from the rest of Germany. In the 1920s, Germany only reluctantly agreed to the continued payment of reparations.

Nazi foreign policy was set in this historical context. But Hitler of course had his own agenda, and it would be wrong to see his policy and actions as simply being determined by German history.

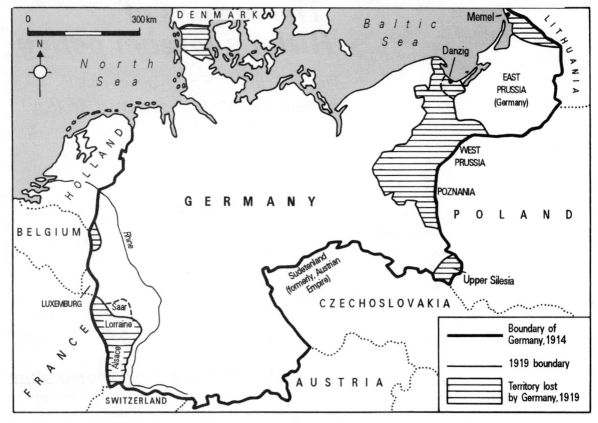

# Nazi foreign policy commitments in 1933

Hitler brought to office both personal and party foreign policy commitments. These were summarised in his autobiography, *Mein Kampf*, a work whose significance has been subjected to widely different interpretations.

## Mein Kampf

This was a book written by Hitler when in prison, following the failure of the Munich Putsch in 1923. The title translates as 'My Struggle', and is a mixture of autobiography, racist authoritarian philosophy and general assertions about the future direction of Nazi policy. Hitler wrote of the need for racial purity within Germany and the need for the German people to be prepared to fight for living space, *Lebensraum*, in Eastern Europe:

> 'Only an adequate large space on this earth assures a nation of freedom of existence ... (We) must find the courage to gather our people and their strength for an advance along the road that will lead this people from its present restricted living space to new land and soil ... We must hold unflinchingly to our aim ... to secure for the German people the land and soil to which they are entitled.'

In the light of what happened later, foreign policy references like this were seen by Churchill and others as giving clear indication that Hitler had at an early stage drawn up a radical plan for domination of Europe. Once in power, he proceeded to carry out this plan quite systematically. This view has been challenged, notably among British historians by A.J.P. Taylor, who saw *Mein Kampf* simply as the daydreaming of a failed revolutionary. These conflicting views are examined more closely in chapter 6 below.

### German expectations

Hitler also had debts to those who had either supported or acquiesced in his gaining power. Above all:

◆ His attacks on those who had betrayed Germany at the end of the First World War and on the shameful Versailles Peace Treaty had raised the expectation that the National Socialists (Nazis) would restore Germany to its rightful place among the European nations.

◆ He could never have become Chancellor without the tacit support of the other right-wing parties in the Weimar Republic. In practice, these parties swiftly became impotent, but their ex-members became enthusiastic supporters of Hitler's enterprising foreign policy.

◆ In 1933 and 1934, the great German industrialists and the bulk of the senior army officers, expecting a Nazi programme of re-armament and military build-up, either supported or agreed to Hitler extending his control.

The Nazi philosophy of totalitarianism saw citizens as subordinate to the needs of the state and expected to contribute to building up its power. Pursuing Germany's international interests was arguably the fundamental purpose of the Nazi state, and a purpose to which ultimately all domestic policy should be directed. Once in power, Hitler was committed to and willingly undertook an active foreign policy which sought to restore Germany's prime position in Europe. German history and Nazi philosophy both required it. Hitler's own fanaticism, and his willingness to act boldly, ensured that the pursuit of his goal would be vigorous.

## International relations before 1933

In the late 1920s, it had seemed that Europe had moved into a new period of stability in international relations. In particular, Germany was beginning to be accepted once more as a respectable European power:

◆ Locarno in 1925 had created a hopeful new framework for international relations. Particularly significant was the agreement that confirmed Germany's frontiers with Belgium and France, including the continued demilitarisation of the Rhineland.

◆ Germany in 1926 became a member of the League of Nations.

◆ The 1928 Kellogg–Briand Pact, which Germany signed, renounced the use of war as an instrument of international relations.

◆ The sixty-nation League disarmament conference, convened in 1932, pointed in the same hopeful direction.

The fragility of this apparent new European accord was exposed from 1933 onwards, though clearly Hitler's actions were not alone responsible for this.

# The international economic crisis after 1929

One element behind the apparent political stability of the late 1920s had been the recovery of European economies and world trade. Nowhere had this been more evident than in Germany itself. There were hints that this happy situation was coming to an end in 1928, but they were brutally overtaken by the world-wide consequences of the 1929 Wall Street Crash. The economic depression, and the mass unemployment which followed, helped bring Hitler to power and then greatly affected the conduct of international relations.

The two most obvious political consequences of the depression were:

◆ A drive for self-sufficiency and growth, which encouraged Germany to direct labour more effectively. This included military conscription and promoted re-armament policies as an answer to unemployment.

◆ The enormous social expenditure and bleak economic prospects at home discouraged firm action in international affairs.

Economic malaise was a major cause of weak French and British foreign policy in the 1930s, and was also at the heart of the new isolationism which encouraged the United States to turn its back on European affairs. Any explanation of the causes of the Second World War must recognise how economic problems encouraged a climate where the drift to war became unstoppable.

## Studying the background to Hitler's foreign policy

**1** Why was Germany's power and central position in Europe a matter of great concern to the other European states? Why did this remain the case after the First World War, despite the harsh terms imposed on Germany in 1919?

**2** Use the map on page 6 and look up the terms imposed on Germany at Versailles. Draw up a list of German grievances at their treatment.

**3** Use a textbook of European history covering Hitler's rise to power to establish the nature of his appeal to so many of the German people, particularly in relation to Germany's position in Europe and its treatment after the First World War. Look up any major references to Hitler's autobiography *Mein Kampf*, but suspend judgement on the significance of *Mein Kampf* until you have read up on the history of the 1930s.

**4** Look up the details of the Locarno Pact of 1925, signed on behalf of the Weimar Republic by Stresemann, the greatest German statesman of the 1920s. He wanted better relations with France and was prepared to make concessions, but was unable to accept the eastern frontiers imposed on Weimar Germany at Versailles. Why?

# 3 Hitler's foreign policy 1933–37

*Did Hitler consciously plan for future German expansion?*

## Key points

◆ Breaking the Treaty of Versailles 1933-35
◆ Hitler becomes bolder 1935-36
◆ Re-militarisation of the Rhineland 1936
◆ Germany's changing foreign relations
◆ Hitler tightens his grip on Germany

## Breaking the Treaty of Versailles 1933-35

By 1932 Germany had retrieved much of its status as a major European power. Hitler's early steps in foreign policy were both cautious and within the Weimar tradition. In these years he had an agenda of 'wrongs' done to Germany in the aftermath of the First World War, which he wished to right. He proved to be a masterly improviser, but he made some serious mistakes.

### Reparations

The Nazis had long denounced reparations as part of the fraudulent Versailles Treaty imposed on Germany. In practice, their payment had already been suspended before Hitler came to power. Hitler's refusal to resume payments, though providing useful propaganda for him within Germany, simply reflected a reality already accepted by the other powers.

### Abandoning disarmament 1933

The disarmament of Germany at Versailles had been seen as the first step towards wider arms reduction, but it was 1932 before a conference assembled to deal with the issue. At this conference, the French proved reluctant to make practical concessions on the balance of arms held, and demanded a four-year delay in the disarmament timetable.

In October 1933 Hitler used this, and the divisions between the French and British on the issue, as an excuse to withdraw Germany from the disarmament conference. This was no empty gesture. German military expenditure in the financial year 1934–35 grew to five times what it had been in 1933–34 (see page 47). For whatever final purpose, Hitler worked at this time to create a German economy that would provide total industrial backing for the German military.

Only days later, Hitler also withdrew Germany from the League of Nations. This repudiation of the legacy of Versailles was overwhelmingly popular in Germany, and was backed by the civil service, diplomats and army commanders. The withdrawal from the League marked a significant change in direction from that previously pursued by Weimar politicians like Stresemann, who had striven to bring Germany back into the international mainstream.

## The Polish Non-Aggression Pact 1934

Hitler moved skilfully and swiftly in arranging the ten-year Non-Aggression Pact, signed with Poland in January 1934. The Pact:

◆ safeguarded Germany's eastern frontier.

◆ helped to undermine the French system of alliances in Eastern Europe by countering the key Franco-Polish alliance of 1925.

◆ suggested to the outside world that Hitler's intentions were essentially peaceful.

It has been argued, notably by Shirer in *The Rise and Fall of the Third Reich*, that even in 1934 this was part of Hitler's master-plan for European domination. 'Before Poland could be obliterated, Hitler saw, it must be separated from its alliance with France.' The Pact was certainly bold in ignoring German popular resentment of Poland, but it had sensible short-term advantages for Germany in protecting its eastern frontier. It seems unlikely that Hitler at this stage envisaged events through to 1939.

## Failure in Austria 1934

An Austrian by birth, Hitler had dreamt in *Mein Kampf* of incorporating Austria into a unified greater German state, a move specifically forbidden by the 1919 peace treaties. When the Austrian Nazis assassinated Chancellor Dolfuss in an attempted coup, Hitler's first reaction was one of delight. But when the Austrian government brutally restored order and Mussolini moved Italian forces to the Austrian border in their support, he quickly took a neutral line. The wish to unite with Austria was partly personal sentiment and partly an expression of a nationalist aspirations for a greater Germany. It was a radical policy, as historically, Austria had always been a separate state from Germany.
    In this episode Hitler was:

◆ improvising his reactions to events rather than pursuing a plan.

◆ in danger of pushing Italy into closer relations with France.

The Austrian policy had not been well-handled. It had proved easier to incite the Austrian Nazis than to control them, and it showed the limits of Germany's power to pursue an ambitious foreign policy in 1934. In these years, Hitler was more absorbed with creating the Nazi state in Germany than he was with foreign policy. In 1935, he grew bolder.

### Plebiscite in the Saar 1935

Early in 1935, as laid down at Versailles in 1919, there was a plebiscite in the Saar. By a nine-to-one majority, the inhabitants voted to be reunited with Germany. This greatly boosted Hitler's prestige. He promptly announced plans to introduce compulsory military service and an extended armaments programme in continued defiance of the Versailles Treaty, using an increase in French military conscription as a pretext. Germany now proposed to have a peacetime army of over half a million men, and for the first time acknowledged that it already possessed an airforce. There was a hint of recklessness about this blatant defiance.

### Reaction outside Germany

Hitler paid a price for his bravado when his political opponents Britain, France and Italy formally protested at this breaking of Versailles. They formed the Stresa Front to resist further encroachments on the Treaty. It seemed likely that Hitler had taken a step too far in his reassertion of Germany's position. He was fortunate that the three powers had made no arrangements as to how the Stresa Front would achieve the objectives. The inept policy of Britain and the territorial ambitions of Italy in any case ensured that the threat to Germany's interests proved both hollow and temporary:

◆ Within a month Britain, without consulting the French, signed an Anglo–German naval agreement which permitted a far bigger German navy than anything agreed at Versailles.

◆ In October 1935, Fascist Italy invaded the territory of Abyssinia, a fellow member of the League of Nations. It was a move which effectively estranged Italy from Britain and France, the two leading League members, over the next year. This in turn opened up a series of new opportunities for German diplomacy.

# Hitler becomes bolder 1936-37

In the three years from his coming to power in January 1933 until the end of 1935, Hitler had asserted Germany's position in Europe more abrasively than his democratic predecessors. He had behaved most radically regarding the fate of Austria, but he had not done so with any clear indication of his future intentions. There was no certain evidence of a desire for war, or of any overall plan for the future. It was open for foreign observers to note that Hitler's actions were justifiable, as they resolved grievances unjustly imposed on Germany at the end of the First World War. In the Austrian debacle of 1934 and with the collapse of the Stresa Front, Hitler had been lucky to avoid the worst possible consequences of his actions. From this good luck and the disunion of potential enemies, he took courage to make his boldest move to date.

### Re-militarising the Rhineland 1936

There were strong domestic reasons why the Nazis, self-proclaimed defenders of Germany's honour, could not ignore the anomaly that the German army was excluded from the Rhineland. Unlike the Saar, the Rhineland was fully part of

Germany under the Versailles arrangements. Re-militarising it was Hitler's riskiest move so far.

The demilitarised Rhineland stood as France's best guarantee against a future attack from Germany. In view of the deep bitterness between the two nations, it seemed unlikely that France would stand by and see the German army move too close to the French border. At some point, Hitler's domestic reputation as an extreme nationalist would have forced him to act. In his favour were the emerging strength of the growing German army and, far more importantly, the divisions among his potential opponents.

Hitler took close interest in the deteriorating relations between Italy, Britain and France over Abyssinia. He moved cautiously, and did not act over the Rhineland until it became clear in 1936 that the Italians were going to win in Abyssinia. Many of his senior generals, including Blomberg his Commander-in-Chief, were still deeply concerned at the risk of French military action against the German forces. The occupation was very much Hitler's own decision. He kept his nerve, promising his generals that he would withdraw at the first sign of French intervention. This proved, as he had predicted, quite unnecessary.

The occupation was totally unopposed. The French, with both politicians and military divided on what to do, would not act alone. The British were unconvinced that armed opposition to the Germans 'occupying their own backyard' was justified. Churchill then, and others later, argued that this was the classic moment when Hitler should have been checked.

## A missed opportunity?

For a long time after the Second World War, it was accepted that decisive military action had been possible against the 10,000 German troops and 23,000 armed police who had moved into the Rhineland. It seemed likely that the German forces would have had to withdraw. Then, more speculatively, Hitler's position in Germany could have become less secure, with perhaps even the army turning against him after the debacle.

But the situation facing the French was almost certainly more complex than this simple analysis suggests, for:

◆ the German army might have offered resistance, and the population almost certainly would have done, as in the Ruhr in 1923.

◆ the French army was not organised for such a campaign and had no plans to implement it. The defensive mentality of the Maginot Line, built from 1929–34, already dominated French military thinking, so that the advice the military gave to the government was confused and defeatist.

◆ arguably the devastation of the First World War had left the French without the will to fight another war. Moreover, the country was in the midst of yet another internal political crisis, with the extremes of Left and Right bitterly divided and with only a caretaker government in control.

◆ French action in the Rhineland may well have cemented support for the Nazi government rather than the opposite.

The prospect of checking Hitler's ambitions at this point now looks more doubtful than it did to those who thought like Churchill at the time or, more frequently, later. In any event, Hitler's personal gamble paid off. His success certainly emboldened him further, opening up a new phase of more reckless assertions of German 'rights'. In the Rhineland on the other hand, the build-up of a German military presence was something of an anti-climax, proceeding very slowly. It had clearly not been planned in advance as part of a more aggressive German military strategy in Western Europe.

# Germany's changing foreign relations

## Germany and Italy

From 1934, the Non-Aggression Pact with Poland had been the key to German security as Hitler flirted with adventures in the west. The divisions among his potential opponents in Western Europe now enabled him to develop German links with Italy which, with its presence in the Mediterranean, would check any resolute action by France. There may not have been a master-plan to this effect, but the diplomatic advantages to Germany were obvious. It is worth noting that all the other European powers consistently overvalued Fascist Italy's powers, and from 1935–39 the ever-closer relations between the two fascist powers were of great advantage to Hitler in helping to neutralise both France and Britain. The Italian invasion of Abyssinia had undermined any prospect of the western states reviving the Stresa Front, for Britain and France did too little to help Abyssinia but enough to antagonise Italy and make Mussolini re-assess the basis of Italian foreign policy.

It was in March 1936, while Italian forces were finally overrunning Abyssinia, that German troops moved into the Rhineland. In the summer, the two states began their joint intervention on the side of Franco's (right-wing) Nationalists in the Spanish Civil War. This revolution in Italian diplomacy was completed and symbolised in the same year by Mussolini's reference to the 'Axis' of Rome and Berlin, around which European affairs would in future revolve.

From that point, Mussolini drew closer and closer to Hitler. At first he was an apparent equal, but by 1939 he was increasingly the ignored junior partner in the Axis. The most immediate loser was Austria, which could no longer rely on Italy's support against any threat from Germany. Hitler's promises to Mussolini that he would respect Austrian independence could easily be evaded or forgotten when the right circumstances arose.

## The Spanish Civil War 1936–39

Germany's involvement in this war, promptly agreed by Hitler and his immediate advisers following a request from the Nationalist leader General Franco, was never on the same scale as Italy. There were, at any time, probably fewer than 10,000 Germans committed in Spain, compared with perhaps 70,000 Italians. The prospect of a right-wing victory in Spain was clearly in the interests of the other right-wing European powers, but Hitler had other motives for his limited intervention:

◆ The prolongation of the war kept Italy's military resources stretched and so kept it more dependent on the new German alliance.

◆ The war added to the diplomatic uncertainties of France and Britain, encouraging the growth of pacifist feeling in those countries and also making any improvement in their relations with Italy impossible.

◆ The war provided an opportunity to test Germany's expanded army and airforce.

German intervention in the war was a useful but minor strand in Hitler's foreign policy in the years 1936–39. German help, especially its aircraft, was important to Franco at key points in the war, but his eventual victory owed more to Spanish factors than foreign intervention.

### The Japanese connection

In November 1936 Germany signed the Anti-Comintern Pact with Japan. In 1937 the Pact was joined by Italy, creating the Rome–Berlin–Tokyo Axis. Hitler and his chief negotiator, Ribbentrop, saw the alliance with the increasingly militaristic Japan as a useful counter in Asia to both the British and the Russians.

Hitler's Japanese alliance was effective in creating problems for potential enemies. After the European war had broken out in 1939, the Japanese were useful to Germany because their ambitions in the Far East continued to distract the United States government from full-scale interference in European affairs. Hitler either failed to note or chose to disregard the prospect that the Japanese alliance might involve complications in Germany's relations with the United States.

### Hitler and Britain 1933–37

In *Mein Kampf* Hitler had seen Britain as Germany's natural ally in the west, and, as late as the Anglo-German naval agreement of 1935, had continued to believe that Britain would be prepared to ally with Germany and accept German domination of the European continent, in return for a free hand overseas. This view of Britain ignored its traditional foreign policy commitment to preventing any one strong power dominating the continent. Hitler's understanding of British policy has as a result been described as fatally flawed. With the formation of the Axis in early 1937, the possibility of a British alliance was over and Germany was firmly aligned with powers hostile to Britain. However, this did not mean that Hitler saw a war with Britain as inevitable at this time.

## Hitler tightens his grip on Gernany

Early in 1938, Hitler's personal control of the army and the conduct of foreign policy were both reinforced in moves which complemented the creation of the Nazi totalitarian state in other areas of German life:

◆ A new high command of the German Armed Forces was created in the *Oberkommando der Wehrmacht* (OKW). It was created by Hitler, separate from the old army hierarchy, to act as his personal staff in a general tightening of Nazi control. The new structure ensured that in military matters it was Hitler's will that prevailed. At this point, he took on the duties of the Commander-in-Chief of the armed forces.

◆ There was then a purge of leading civil servants in the foreign office, including the removal of several independently-minded ambassadors. The main beneficiary was the fanatical Nazi, Ribbentrop, who became Foreign Minister and a central figure in German foreign policy in the critical years 1938–39. From here on, there was no one of importance to query Hitler's conduct of foreign policy.

## Studying Hitler's foreign policy from 1933–37

**1** Consult the time-chart in the Reference Section. Then look again at the post-1919 map of Europe on page 6. Note the position of the Rhineland and the relative positions of Germany, France, Austria, Poland and Italy. This will help you to follow the often complex issues at stake between them.

**2** Think about what the failed coup of 1934 in Austria reveals about Hitler's foreign policy. Relate his actions to the claims on Austria that he had made in *Mein Kampf* and to the formation of the Stresa Front. Why did the solitary attempt of the Stresa Front to combine against the threat from Nazi Germany collapse so suddenly and so totally?

**3** Be ready to explain the importance for Hitler of his agreements in these years with both Poland and Italy, and why Nazi Germany moved into a closer relationship with Japan.

**4** Construct a one-paragraph statement on why the re-militarisation of the Rhineland is often seen as the best moment to have checked Hitler without a major conflict. List the reasons why recent historians have wondered whether this was really the case.

**5** In *Mein Kampf*, Hitler saw Britain as the natural ally for Germany. By 1937, this dream was dead. Try to explain why this had happened.

# 4 *A greater Reich*

## *German expansion in 1938*

---

### Key points

- ◆ *Anschluss*, March 1938
- ◆ Crisis in the Sudetenland
- ◆ The build-up to negotiations
- ◆ The Munich Agreement, September 1938

---

## Anschluss, March 1938

The idea of union (*Anschluss*) between Austria and Germany had been specifically forbidden in the 1919 Versailles Treaty. But by 1938 the obstacles to
*Anschluss* had weakened:

- ◆ France, which had blocked a proposed customs union between Germany
  and Austria in 1931, had failed to act over the re-militarisation of the
  Rhineland, where its national interests were far more directly involved. It
  could now perhaps be disregarded.

- ◆ Britain had indicated no opposition to the development of closer ties
  between the two countries, providing this happened legally and gradually.

- ◆ Most importantly Italy, which had prevented Hitler exploiting the 1934
  Austrian crisis, was now too committed in the Spanish Civil War to act
  decisively in another area. Italy was in any event now allied to Germany.

Evidence of Austrian Nazi plotting against the state had alarmed the Austrian
Chancellor Schuschnigg. Hitler agreed to meet Schuschnigg at Berchtesgaden
in Germany, where he took advantage of the situation to bully Schuschnigg
into accepting the Austrian Nazis into government and releasing Nazi prison-
ers, some of whom had been held since the 1934 coup. With little effort on
Hitler's part, Austria seemed destined to slip easily into subservience to the
much larger German state.

The Austrian Nazis, led by Seyss-Inquart, continued agitating and plotting
to seize power in Austria. The decision of Schuschnigg to call their bluff by
holding a referendum on the issue of Austria's continuing independence com-
pelled Hitler to involve himself again in Austrian affairs. Had Hitler not
become involved, the referendum may have strengthened Schussnigg, setting
him free from his agreement with Hitler. A major obstacle would have been
placed in the way of *Anschluss* in the future.

Unable to risk an anti-union vote, Hitler closed the German border with Austria and began to exert pressure through the right-wing members of the Austrian parliament, who demanded that the referendum be cancelled and Schussnigg be replaced as Chancellor by Seyss-Inquart. The latter formed a provisional government of doubtful legality, and invited the German army to enter the country to protect law and order. German Nazi pressure was at the heart of the take-over of the Austrian Government. It was Goering who threatened the Austrian President, Miklas, with a German invasion unless Schussnigg was allowed to resign. Goering also dictated the telegram in which Seyss-Inquart invited the Germans into the country.

On 12 March, the German army received a rapturous welcome from the Austrian people. On entering Austria, Hitler too received an ecstatic welcome, and was swept away by the general enthusiasm. On 13 March, Seyss-Inquart declared the union of the two countries. Hitler's initial idea of a puppet Austrian Nazi government was hastily abandoned and *Anschluss* became an unopposed reality, creating a Greater Germany of 70 million inhabitants.

## European consequences

Since 1934, Hitler's dream of a united greater German nation had hardened into a definite intention. But in 1938 its timing and its precise form were the result of inspired improvisation. It is going too far to suggest that *Anschluss* came about by accident, for Hitler had actively encouraged the internal Nazi pressure on the Austrian state and had browbeaten Schussnigg disgracefully. His diplomatic methods lacked subtlety and grace, but he had proved a shrewd calculator of risks. In plebiscites in both Austria and Germany, *Anschluss* was welcomed by

**Figure 2**
Map of German expansion, March 1938 – March 1939

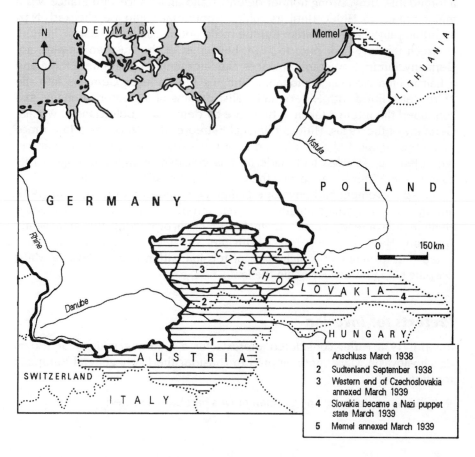

| | |
|---|---|
| 1 | Anschluss March 1938 |
| 2 | Sudtenland September 1938 |
| 3 | Western end of Czechoslovakia annexed March 1939 |
| 4 | Slovakia became a Nazi puppet state March 1939 |
| 5 | Memel annexed March 1939 |

over 99% of the voters. Italy accepted the fait accompli and the French were again between governments. The British government limited itself to formal protests about the methods employed, for there were no serious British interests involved. For many, it was seen as a purely German affair.

However, the consequences for Europe were immense:

◆ Hitler's triumph caught the imagination of the German people and his personal prestige soared.

◆ The easy acceptance of Anschluss by Britain and France strengthened Hitler's self-confidence in his own ability to assess foreign policy issues and conduct Germany's international affairs, just at the point when his tightened grip over the German army and civil service took effect.

◆ Germany now had common frontiers with Italy, Hungary and Yugoslavia which, together with its control of Vienna and the middle reaches of the River Danube, greatly extended German economic dominance of South-Eastern Europe.

◆ The heavily fortified Czech western frontier with Germany was outflanked and Czechoslovakia was open to German pressure.

Those who saw Anschluss as a purely German affair were deluding themselves.

# Crisis in the Sudetenland

Czechoslovakia's existence in Central Europe as a multi-racial democracy with a formidable army, strong frontier defences and an alliance with France was a major irritant to Hitler. Until its military potential could be checked, Nazi ambitions anywhere in Eastern Europe could not be safely pursued.

Czech territory had, prior to 1914, been part of the Austrian Empire, not Germany. But in its western provinces, the Sudetenland, there were three and a half million German inhabitants. Bringing the Sudeten Germans into the Third Reich fitted with Hitler's nationalist dreams of a greater Germany, and continued the interest taken in their fate by democratic politicians of Weimar Germany of the 1920s. Hitler's personal hatred of the Czechs as a lower race made the prospect of action to end their rule over so many Germans particularly pleasing. Anschluss had made all this possible. Within a fortnight of its completion, Hitler began to give the Czech problem his full attention.

A Nazi movement had developed among the Sudeten Germans after 1933, and the end of Austria strengthened their ambitions. In 1937, the Nazi leader Henlein had already come out in favour of incorporating the area within Germany. He was in close touch with the Nazi leadership in Berlin, which urged him to maintain a high state of tension within Czechoslovakia whilst keeping his agitation just within the law.

### Pretexts for invasion

In April 1938 Hitler considered pretexts for a lightning military attack on Czechoslovakia. Once more, he had to consider the likely general European reaction:

◆ Italian acceptance of any German moves had been assured.

◆ The 1934 Non-Aggression Pact with Poland and that state's own territorial ambitions over land in eastern Czechoslovakia should ensure Polish acceptance, however short-sighted, of any German moves.

◆ The Little Entente of smaller east European states (Czechoslovakia, Romania and Yugoslavia), formed in the 1920s to resist any German expansion in the region, had already disintegrated. In 1937 both Romania and Yugoslavia had been unwilling to pledge military aid to the Czechs in the event of a German attack on them.

◆ French alliances with each of the members of the Little Entente had been undermined by the Little Entente's collapse. France had twice accepted German expansionism without making a move, and its interests in the Sudetenland were indirect.

◆ The Soviet Union had, in 1935, signed a defence pact with Czechoslovakia, though with the proviso that their obligations only came into effect if the French honoured their commitments to the Czechs.

◆ Britain had no military commitments to the Czechs.

◆ The Czechs had no common frontiers with friendly countries and so the obstacles to anyone trying to help them would be formidable.

Hitler believed that he could discount the Soviet Union, as it was deeply immersed in its own internal purges. He also appeared to believe that in practice, both Britain and France had already written off Czechoslovakia. In this, he was wrong. Chamberlain, the British Prime Minister, was to become deeply involved in trying to solve the Czech problem.

### An unclear strategy

Hitler's strategy was at this stage unclear, perhaps even to himself. He may have wanted the glory of an easy military victory over the Czechs, and was certainly enraged by Czech defiance in May 1938 when the Czech President Benes ordered partial mobilisation of his army in response to rumours of threatening German troop movements. On the other hand, Hitler may have assumed that the Czechs would, like the Austrian Government, cave in to German demands when faced with further bullying tactics by the larger nation. At this point however Hitler lost the initiative, temporarily, to Chamberlain.

# The build-up to negotiations

Following *Anschluss*, Chamberlain had convinced himself that if a general war was to be avoided, it was essential that the Czechs make concessions to the Germans on the Sudeten issue. The French were only too anxious to follow the British lead which, if successful, would allow them to evade the clear military commitments of their Little Entente alliance with the Czechs.

It was relatively easy to be convinced that the German case had merit. The large German minority had been placed within the new state of Czechoslovakia at the 1919 Paris Peace Conference in order to make it territorially and economically viable, but without the occupants' own wishes being taken into account. The Nazis under Henlein argued that the Sudetenland Germans had been denied any opportunity of being consulted on their fate.

**Figure 3**
The Czech Crisis.
This *News of the World*
cartoon from
25 September 1938
captured the drama of
Chamberlain's efforts to
push the world back from
chaos and war to peace.

Once more, the evident rough justice meted out at the Paris Peace Conference could be exploited by Hitler to create doubts and divisions among potential opponents. Throughout the crisis which now emerged, Chamberlain was certainly far more aware of German grievances than those of the Czechs.

## Avoiding conflict

Hitler had everything to gain by keeping the tension high. This he did in masterly fashion across the summer of 1938, culminating in a savage attack on the Czechs in a speech to the German Nazi rally at Nuremberg, which was broadcast across Europe on 12 September. Hitler's repeated hints of a deadline, after which he would act, screwed the tension still higher. Many in Europe waited for the outbreak of a general war.

Chamberlain, seeking to avoid conflict through negotiation and compromise, flew to meet Hitler at Berchtesgaden on 15 September 1938. He immediately agreed to accept the principle of self-determination by the inhabitants of the Sudetenland as the basis for re-drawing the frontiers of Germany and Czechoslovakia, so long as Hitler did not attack the Czechs before the proposal could be formally agreed by the British government. Hitler, very unimpressed by Chamberlain's appearance and diplomatic approach, agreed to this proviso, for he intended no action before October.

Chamberlain's visit and ready concessions had removed any lingering fear of Hitler's that Britain and France would intervene in any action Germany took in the Sudetenland. On his second visit to Hitler at Godesberg on 22 September, Chamberlain brought the British and French governments' agreement that any Sudeten areas where more than 50% of the people were German would be handed over to Germany without even the formality of a plebiscite. This simply confirmed Hitler's view that he had a free hand to bring further pressure on the Czechs. Contacts between British and German diplomats reinforced this opinion. The Czechs had been humiliated by their only potential allies. President Benes was, under protest, forced by British and French pressure to agree to the proposals brokered by Chamberlain.

Hitler's intransigence at this point goes a long way to justifying the arguments of those who regarded each concession as feeding Hitler's appetite. It offers strong support for those historians who argue that both Hitler's ambitious territorial dreams and his aggressive conduct of foreign policy contributed crucially to the deterioration in international relations which led, just a year later, to the outbreak of war.

## Hitler takes the initiative

Hitler's reaction to the proposals put to him on 22 September was to reject what was offered, on the grounds that it would take too long to implement. He instead demanded that the German army be allowed to take over the Sudetenland within two days, where he falsely alleged massacres of German civilians were taking place. He then made much out of his concession to wait until 1 October before moving his army in. At this meeting, Hitler also demanded that the Czechs should meet the territorial claims of the Poles and the Hungarians on their eastern and southern frontiers.

Benes now rebelled against the Anglo-French pressure. He rejected Hitler's new terms and ordered military mobilisation. In both Paris and London, war seemed the likeliest outcome as the German propaganda machine kept the pressure on the Czechs. In a public broadcast speech on 26 September, Hitler gave the Czechs just 24 hours in which to agree to hand over the Sudetenland to Germany before 1 October.

## Doubts set in

At this stage Hitler was still assuming that France and Britain would take no retaliatory action. He could have his local war against the Czechs and the military glory that would surely follow. Then doubts set in, for the French had called up reserve troops and sections of the British fleet had put to sea. There were divisions among Hitler's ministers, and it seemed that, despite all the warlike Nazi propaganda, the population of Berlin was not filled with enthusiasm at the prospect of war.

Chamberlain urged Mussolini to use his good relations with Hitler to arrange another meeting. Hitler's new doubts meant that he reluctantly agreed to Mussolini's proposal for a third meeting with Chamberlain, where he was also to meet Daladier, the French Prime Minister. This meeting of the leaders of Britain, France, Germany and Italy, but not the Czechs or the Russians, would take place at Munich on 29 September, just two days ahead of Hitler's deadline. Tension across Europe could scarcely have been higher.

## The Munich Agreement, September 1938

At Munich, the British and the French quickly agreed to the German military occupation of the Sudetenland from 1–10 October. They also agreed to the Hungarian and Polish demands for territory. The Czechs were told that they either accepted the terms negotiated by their allies, or they fought alone. Once they had accepted, there was a weak guarantee by the four Munich powers to respect the territorial integrity of what was left of the Czechoslovak state.

In, for Hitler, a meaningless postscript to the meetings, Chamberlain secured a jointly-signed declaration that Britain and Germany were resolved never to go to war again, but always to negotiate their differences. It has been claimed that Hitler scarcely read the few lines on which Chamberlain set so much store and which he waved so enthusiastically to those who welcomed him home to Britain. In Germany Hitler's prestige was higher than it had ever been, for in foreign affairs he seemed unable to put a foot wrong. The Czechs had lost their border defences and vital industrial areas, and Benes resigned as President. The rump of the state left after Munich began to disintegrate within a new federal structure, and would be easy prey for Hitler in the future.

Hitler had been handed all he had demanded on a plate. But perhaps, according to his later words, to his secret chagrin he had been denied the sweet fruits of a military victory over the Czechs and the prospect of a victory march through Prague.

## Studying the events of 1938

**1** Rehearse the arguments why so many Britons thought it was reasonable for Germany and Austria to unite. Why did they wish to take this line? What were the legal obstacles to such unification? Be ready to explain why *Anschluss* fitted so well into Hitler's racial and nationalist policies.

**2** Why did *Anschluss* fail in 1934, but succeed in 1938? Be ready to explain what was different, both within Austria and Germany and internationally.

**3** How would you briefly explain the strategic consequences of *Anschluss* for Czechoslovakia?

**4** Use the index or contents list of a standard textbook to look up the entries on Chamberlain and on appeasement. Make a simple time-chart of the events of the Munich crisis. Construct very brief statements on why at Munich:
- Chamberlain could feel that he was saving Europe from catastrophe.
- the Czechs felt betrayed.
- the Soviet Union could feel slighted and dangerously isolated.
- Hitler felt cheated.
- Hitler came to despise the leaders of Britain and France.

# 5 The final steps to war 1938–39

*A pattern of conquest or a miscalculation?*

---

## Key points

◆ Occupation of Czechoslovakia, 1938
◆ The question of Poland
◆ The Soviet Union: the Nazi–Soviet Pact, 23 August 1939
◆ War in Europe

---

## Occupation of Czechoslovakia, 1938

Within days of the Munich Agreement, Hitler had military plans for a surprise attack on the remains of Czechoslovakia. After Munich, the separatist demands of the Slovaks seriously weakened the authority of the Prague government. The new president, Hacha, had to agree to a federal constitution which virtually turned the country into two separate states. Hitler certainly encouraged the continuing demands of the Slovak leaders for complete independence, which they declared in March 1939. The plight of the abandoned Czechs was most vividly illustrated by President Hacha, who turned to Hitler for help in preserving the remnants of the Czech state.

Hacha, an old man, was subjected to immense pressure when, at his own request, he went to Berlin. He probably took the only option when he handed over the remaining Czech provinces, Bohemia and Moravia, to German protection, for Prague was under threat of aerial bombardment if he did not do so. German troops then marched into Prague. On 16 March 1939 Hitler incorporated the Czech provinces into Nazi Germany, with Slovakia becoming a Nazi puppet state.

Hitler's talented touch in foreign affairs had apparently not deserted him, for France and Britain made only muted protests at this flagrant breach of the arrangements agreed so recently at Munich. Action to help the Czechs was by now well beyond their capability. And yet, in his delight at this further expansion of German territory, Hitler failed to note the effect that this further advance of German power had on foreign opinion, particularly in Britain where the policy of appeasement was discredited almost overnight. It now became a common belief that Hitler and the Germans could not be trusted.

### Memel

The Baltic city of Memel had once been in the German province of East Prussia, but was made a free city in 1919 and seized by Lithuania in 1923. It had a largely German population, among whom a fiercely nationalistic Nazi movement had developed and gained control of the city council. In March 1939, they invited Hitler to take control of the city. German troops entered the area less than a week after they had occupied Prague. There was nothing Lithuania could do other than accept the fact of the German occupation.

A.J.P. Taylor later saw the Memel episode as the result of a spontaneous local German uprising, provoked by excitement over the German occupation of Prague, to which Hitler simply improvised a response. In France and Britain it simply helped to confirm the growing feeling that Hitler could not be trusted. He was clearly embarking on a campaign of annexations that would only end with German domination of the European continent.

# The question of Poland

The new mood in Britain was reflected in even Chamberlain's speeches in the Commons. In April, Britain made guarantees of support for Poland if it were attacked. These were in turn extended jointly by France and Britain to both Greece and Romania. The British assurances of support if Polish independence were threatened were offered unconditionally, and the Polish Foreign Minister, Beck, was given a free hand in his relations with Germany.

Arguing that Britain could hardly retain any international credibility by abandoning the Poles as it had the Czechs, A.J.P. Taylor in 1961 saw this general guarantee of support, so easily given, as the moment when Britain became committed to military action on the continent. At the time, it all made little impression on Hitler, who was now lured into his most fateful series of decisions.

## Danzig and the Polish Corridor

The Polish Corridor was a strip of Polish territory which separated the German province of East Prussia from the rest of Germany. It had been created by the peacemakers in 1919 in order to provide the newly restored state of Poland with access to the Baltic Sea. At its seaward end was the port of Danzig, which was made a free city under the control of the League of Nations. The vast majority of the inhabitants of the city were German, and since 1933 a strong Nazi movement had grown up in Danzig. It was this presence that Hitler now prepared to exploit, in order to remedy what even democratic Germans of the Weimar Republic era had held to be one of the greatest injustices perpetrated at Versailles. What Hitler sought was the incorporation of Danzig into his Third Reich. He also wanted a German-controlled route to East Prussia across the Polish Corridor.

This may have been the prelude to further demands against Poland. But it was not as outrageous a proposal nor as extensive an expansion of German dominance as those Hitler had already got away with in Austria and Czechoslovakia. During the winter of 1938–39, Hitler had hoped that he could negotiate a deal with the Poles by offering them the possibility of compensating gains in the Soviet Ukraine. But the Polish right-wing government was too fearful of the likely Soviet response to become involved in such a deal with the Germans.

The new British resolve to block any further expansion caused attitudes to harden on both sides, and marked a significant step towards a general war.

British guarantees of aid and the almost simultaneous renewal of the French commitments had two consequences:

◆ They made the Poles less inclined to bow to continuing pressure from Germany and the Polish government more determined to make no concessions on Danzig or the Corridor.

◆ They confirmed Hitler's developing realisation that, if he was to achieve his goals, Polish military power would have to be crushed. In April 1939, he repudiated the 1934 German Non-Aggression Pact with Poland and the 1935 Anglo-German naval agreement.

Few in Britain and France gave any thought on how they were to give practical help to the Poles if the Germans did invade the country. In this, the Poles were as guilty as the French and the British. They criticised the failure of their allies to provide funds for strengthening Polish defences, but were themselves determined to resist Western pressure to give entry to Poland to Soviet forces, who could help to counter the German threat. For the right-wing Polish government, the Soviet Union posed as great a potential threat to Polish integrity as did Nazi Germany.

## The Soviet Union

The Soviet Union had been excluded from the Munich Agreement, despite the fact that they as much as the French had made defensive deals with the Czechs. France and Britain were not willing to form alliances with the communist state, so long excluded from European affairs, whose revolutionary motives were still suspect to most democratic leaders. One of Hitler's attractions for right-wing politicians across Europe was that Nazi Germany would be the best possible ideological and geographical bulwark against the expansion of communism. Nor, if war were to come with Germany, did western military experts place much value on any help from the Soviet Red Army, torn as it was by ruthless purges of its officer corps.

**Figure 4**
'What, no chair for me?'
The Soviet Union was not invited to Munich in September 1938 to discuss the fate of Czechoslovakia. In this cartoon from the *Evening Standard* on 30 September 1938, Stalin is shown putting an inconvenient question to (from left) Hitler, Chamberlain, Daladier and Mussolini. Note the map of Czechoslovakia on the wall.

## The West negotiates

Nevertheless, faced with the obvious prospect of further Nazi expansion after the fall of Prague, this time at the expense of Poland, the French and the British opened cautious negotiations with the Soviets. The Western Powers gave remarkably low priority to the negotiations, which in consequence made very little progress. The British were wary of entering military discussions until the political ground had been cleared. The French were more anxious to secure a Soviet military commitment, and tried to push the reluctant British along. The Soviet Union suspected the motives of both of the other powers, and believed that their real intention was to lure the Soviet Union into fighting their war for them.

The talks stalled on the crucial issue, bluntly posed by the Soviet representatives, of whether the Red Army would be given uninterrupted passage across Poland and Romania in order to engage the German forces. Because of the obstinacy of the Poles, neither the British nor the French representatives could give any commitment on this, though the French were more prepared, if necessary, to force the Poles into agreement in order to secure the Soviets as allies. By May 1939 it had become clear to the Soviets that the Western Powers had little to offer them in the way of their own security, which might well be better served by a deal with Germany. This was the price Britain and France paid for their policies at Munich, and for their inability to put pressure on the Poles.

In the spring of 1939, Hitler became increasingly certain that he would have to take decisive action against Poland. He began building diplomatic bridges with the smaller Eastern European nations of Bulgaria, Hungary and Yugoslavia, and signed non-aggression pacts with the three Baltic republics of Estonia, Latvia and Lithuania. His approach in all this was careful and methodical, and the eventual attack on Poland should not be seen as some rash, inexplicable adventure. It was also at this time, May 1939, that Germany entered into the Pact of Steel with Italy. The ground was being well prepared, and the startling development on 23 August needs to be seen in that context.

## The Nazi–Soviet Pact, 23 August 1939

The first move to foster Soviet–German relations came from Germany on 14 August, with a telegraphed offer that Ribbentrop, the Foreign Minister, could go to Moscow. The absence of any serious issues between the two countries was stressed in this dramatic new move. The Soviets replied cautiously to this overture, even though the Foreign Minister Litvinov, a fiercely anti-Nazi Jew, had been replaced on 3 May by the more agnostic Molotov. For the moment, Molotov maintained the negotiations with Britain and France at their usual slow pace. German pressure on the Soviet government for an early visit by Ribbentrop culminated in a personal message from Hitler to Stalin, asking that Ribbentrop should be received in Moscow immediately.

Despite the ideological gap between the German Nazis and the Russian communists, Hitler saw many advantages in reaching an understanding with them. His 1934 pact with Poland had been obtained in order to provide security on Germany's eastern frontier whilst problems in the west were attended to, but Hitler had never hidden his contempt for the Poles as a lesser race, nor had he forgotten the German lands which had been given to Poland by the Allies in 1919. Once it became clear that his attempts to do a deal with the

Poles were not going to work, the tactical attractions of an understanding with the Soviet Union became evident. Both Germany and the Soviet Union had lost lands to Poland after the First World War, and joint action against the Poles had much to commend it.

The German negotiators went to Moscow, led by Ribbentrop. They made swifter progress than had their British and French counterparts. The early negotiations involved trade agreements between the two countries, which had been signed on 19 August as a preliminary to Ribbentrop's arrival, and included German loans for equipment to build up Soviet industry.

**Figure 5**
This famous cartoon by Low summed up British amazement at the unlikely alliance of the Nazi-Soviet Pact, as the Nazis and the Soviets were political enemies.

On 23 August, the balance of power in Europe was turned upside down when Ribbentrop and Molotov, with Stalin looking on, signed the Nazi–Soviet Non-Aggression Pact. They both pledged that, for the next ten years, they would remain neutral if the other attacked a third power.

Secret clauses in the treaty, news of which only emerged long after the end of the Second World War, drew a new map of Poland divided into Soviet and German 'spheres of influence'. The independent state of Lithuania was to be in the German sphere of influence, and Latvia and Estonia in the Soviet sphere. The Germans also gave the Soviets a free hand to regain the province of Bessarabia from Romania. In the next two years, arrangements made for economic co-operation between the two countries were to provide Germany with invaluable iron ore and oil supplies. In return, Stalin had gained the opportunity to re-acquire most of the Russian lands lost in the aftermath of the First World War.

Hitler can be accused of misreading the new resolution that had begun to emerge in Britain and France after his seizure of Prague. But this German deal with Stalin surely entitled him to assume that the Western Powers would now recognise that they could not honour their commitments to Poland.

## War in Europe

The German negotiations with the Soviet Union had been conducted by Ribbentrop, but Hitler had been closely involved in the momentous shift in foreign policy which they represented. The speed with which events unfolded once the Nazi-Soviet Pact was concluded deserves day-by-day analysis.

**Tuesday 22 August:** Even before the Pact was signed, Hitler was confident that Britain and France had been neutered. He met his military leaders to discuss moves against Poland.

**Wednesday 23 August:** The Pact was signed. Hitler fixed 26 August for the German attack on Poland.

**Thursday 24 August:** Hitler welcomed back Ribbentrop to Berlin as the hero of the hour.

**Friday 25 August:** Britain and France declared that, despite the Pact, they stood by their commitments to Poland. The Anglo-Polish Alliance was signed. Italy indicated that it was not ready to enter a general European war. Hitler told the British Government that he would guarantee the security of the British Empire in return for being allowed to solve the Danzig problem. Henderson, the British ambassador in Berlin, clearly gave Hitler the impression that Britain would be easily cowed into either forcing concessions from Poland or into abandoning the Poles to their fate.

**Monday 28 August:** Britain stated that it stood by its alliance with Poland, and urged negotiations over Danzig. This was taken by Hitler as another indication that the Poles would be pressed to make concessions, as the Czechs had been a year earlier.

**Tuesday 29 August:** Hitler offered to receive a Polish plenipotentiary (representative with full powers) in Berlin to negotiate. Beck, the Polish Foreign Minister, rejected the offer of negotiations, citing the treatment of Czech President Hacha on a similar mission to Berlin, and mobilised Poland's armed forces.

**Friday 1 September:** After staging fake border incidents with German troops dressed in Polish uniforms, the German army invaded Poland. German Nazis drove the League of Nations High Commissioner out of Danzig, and declared it to be part of Germany. At separate meetings with Ribbentrop, the British and the French ambassadors in Berlin warned that unless they received satisfactory German assurances that aggressive action against the Poles had ceased and that German troops were prepared to withdraw promptly from Poland, both countries would 'without hesitation' fulfil their obligation to Poland.

**Sunday 3 September:** After two days' delay, largely because the French wanted time to mobilise rather than in any hope of altering the outcome, Britain declared war on Germany. A few hours later, France followed suit.

Throughout the last days of August, Hitler had expected the Poles eventually to negotiate. His role was to keep the pressure on the Polish government and try to divide it from its allies. In doing so he became committed to preparing for a full-scale attack on Poland. Originally intended for 1 September, the attack was brought forward to 26 August, only to be postponed hours before the deadline. This may well have been Hitler's way of deliberately heightening the tension. The frantic discussions among Poland's allies were well known to Hitler, who had the Berlin telephone system tapped.

However, the Poles seemed to be immune to pressure. Their Foreign Minister, Beck, and their ambassador in Berlin, Lipski, were both convinced that Hitler was bluffing and, in Taylor's memorable phrase, 'kept their nerve unbroken to the last'. With no Polish plenipotentiary with whom to negotiate, at midday on 31 August Hitler gave the order for Poland to be attacked the next day. More conciliatory sounds later that day from the Polish ambassador about the possibility of negotiations came too late.

Hitler had already postponed the attack once. He either could not or was not prepared to do so again. Instead, he gambled that once the German attack began, Poland would stand alone. The weakness of the British and French governments and their representatives had encouraged him in this belief. He received poor intelligence information on the changing political mood in Britain and France, and failed to understand that the two governments were realising that Poland's fate also involved their own status as great powers. His personal pride in his ability to interpret the international mood had grown with each diplomatic success. This, together with a desire for military success to crown his Nazi regime, strengthened his resolve. At dawn on the 1st September, the German army crossed the Polish frontier in force. Shortly afterwards, large formations of German planes dropped bombs across Warsaw.

## Studying the events of 1938–39

**1** Look at the map on page 17. Note the absorption of western Czech lands, including Prague, into the Third Reich, with Slovakia from March 1939 surviving only as a German puppet state. Note also, on Germany's eastern frontier, the Polish Corridor and the situations of Memel and Danzig. Remind yourself of the status of these lands both prior to and after the Versailles Peace Settlement.

**2** Think through how you would explain the change in British and French government attitudes to Hitler, from the high point of appeasement at Munich in September 1938 through to their commitment to stand by Poland if Germany attacked it. Why was appeasement, which had been so attractive an option in 1938, now abandoned?

**3** Construct a one- or two-paragraph statement on why the Nazi–Soviet Pact was so startling an event for Britain and France. Consider whether it should have been such a surprise. Think through what first Hitler and then Stalin hoped to gain from their deal.

**4** Explain why Hitler miscalculated British and French intentions when he attacked Poland. Was he growing increasingly reckless? Did Britain and France fail to make their intentions clear? What part did their conduct over Czechoslovakia play in misleading Hitler? How far would you agree that Germany had a good case over Danzig, and that the Polish Corridor issue was capable of being resolved peacefully?

**5** Imagine yourself facing an essay which requires you to comment on the argument that, because of Poland's attitude to Germany since 1934, its actions at the time of Munich, its refusal to co-operate with the Soviet Union and its refusal to compromise with Germany in 1939, Poland must take a large measure of responsibility for the outbreak of war.

**6** As a revision exercise, make a list of the countries involved in the events of August and September 1939. Consider what you would say about the responsibility of each for the outbreak of war. Then focus on Hitler, and write the final paragraph of an essay which asked you to assess his personal responsibility for the war.

# 6 *Interpreting the origins of the Second World War*

*A vigorous debate*

---

## Key points

◆ The early views: Hitler's master-plan
◆ Taylor's view: Hitler the opportunist
◆ The modern debate

---

## The early views: Hitler's master-plan

### Churchill

The earliest explanation of how events in the 1930s culminated in a general European war came from Winston Churchill, whose book *The Second World War: Volume One, The Gathering Storm* was published in 1948. Its first 358 pages concern events from 1919 to the moment when war began between Britain and Germany, with a devastating attack on the policies of the British and French governments during the 1930s. Churchill assumed it was self-evident that Hitler had had a master-plan to bring about German domination of Europe, which he pursued relentlessly from the moment he came to power in 1933. Churchill provided a brief summary of the essence of Hitler's autobiography *Mein Kampf*, in which he identified the 'granite pillars' of Hitler's policy as the need to gather all the scattered German elements in Europe within a German Empire, and the acquisition of land in Eastern Europe by force. The central purpose of Nazism was to turn the nation into a fighting unit based on racial purity. Foreign policy was to be realistic and ruthless, with Germany singling out its enemies and attacking each in turn.

Churchill saw the events of 1935 as marking the key moment in the drift to war. Looking at the situation just prior to Germany's re-militarisation of the Rhineland, he pointed out that once Germany had been allowed to re-arm by the Allies, 'a second World War was almost certain'. He went on to describe Hitler as 'free to strike'. By this argument, Germany could have been stopped in 1935, but with this lost opportunity there was 'little hope of averting war'.

In Churchill's analysis:

◆ there was a sense of total commitment on Hitler's side, which contrasted completely with the purposelessness of the British government.

◆ the re-militarisation of the Rhineland, the 'rape' of Austria and the 'tragedy' of Czechoslovakia at Munich all followed a pattern worked out in advance by Hitler, and rested on systematic German re-armament intended to prepare the country for war.

◆ once Czechoslovakia had finally been disposed of, Hitler was seen as preparing for 'the forcible settlement of the dispute with Poland over Danzig as a preliminary to the assault on Poland itself'.

Churchill's was a vivid historical account, which the course of events in 1938–39 and beyond seemed to substantiate fully. It remained unchallenged in either broad sweep or in detail for over a decade. In the 1950s and 1960s, distinguished British historians like E.H. Carr, Sir Lewis Namier, Hugh Trevor Roper and Elizabeth Wiskemann also saw Hitler as pursuing a systematic policy of German expansionism. The thrust of this could be seen in *Mein Kampf*, in which the notion of a general European war was acceptable, perhaps even desirable.

### Shirer

The most detailed popular analysis of German domestic history and foreign policy in the Nazi era came from the American reporter and later historian Shirer, who had lived in Germany from 1933 to 1941. In his monumental *The Rise and Fall of the Third Reich* (1960), Shirer too saw a planned Nazi commitment to expansionism that did not shirk from the use of force as an instrument of policy. He presented a purposeful foreign policy, in which the international crises of 1936–39 came about because Hitler wanted them to. Earlier, from 1933 to 1935, Shirer saw Hitler's policy as 'To talk peace, to prepare secretly for war and to proceed with enough caution in foreign policy and clandestine re-armament to avoid any preventative military action against Germany by the Versailles powers' (p345).

The tone of writing is often loaded. Concerning *Anschluss*, Shirer wrote: 'And so Austria, as Austria, passed for the moment out of history, its very name suppressed by the revengeful Austrian who had now joined it to Germany' (p430). The events from May to September 1938, leading to the Munich Agreement, are presented as master-minded by Hitler, whose clear plans included the destruction of Czechoslovakia. In May he is described as 'brooding fitfully' with a 'fury all the more intense' when these plans were checked. The relief of the other powers at this lesson for the German leader attracts the comment: 'Little did those statesmen know the Nazi dictator' (p446).

Shirer's account of the events of late August 1939, prior to the German attack on Poland, reads as a record of double-dealing. The German regime was seen as bent on war, setting up traps for the British and French governments and proposing unreasonable deadlines and conditions on the Poles until the charade of the final excuse for the invasion.

## Taylor's view: Hitler the opportunist

### A.J.P. Taylor

In 1961, A.J.P. Taylor's *The Origins of the Second World War* was published. It attracted much attention and controversy. To get the flavour of the argument, and to sample one of the great works of history written in the second half of the twentieth century, it is useful to look at the subsequent paperback edition (published 1964). In the introduction to this edition, Taylor defended his thesis against those who had challenged it.

Taylor directly challenged the popular views argued by Churchill and other historians. He analysed the successive international crises of the 1930s, and developed the argument that Hitler in practice had no plan for German expansion or European domination, but simply exploited opportunities presented to him by the other European powers. When the European war came in September 1939, it was because Hitler had miscalculated the reactions of Britain and France to the crisis he had created by putting pressure on Poland.

Taylor dismissed the apparently potent revelations of long-term planning in *Mein Kampf* as the dreams of a frustrated revolutionary. He argued that Hitler's ambitions in foreign policy, far from being revolutionary, were only a general re-statement of those traditional German aims realised at the 1918 Treaty of Brest–Litovsk. The notion that *Mein Kampf* provided a blueprint for Nazi foreign policy was, Taylor argued, untenable.

## The Hossbach Memorandum

In November 1937, a meeting was called to review German policy at home and abroad. It was attended by Hitler, the heads of the armed forces and top Foreign Ministry officials, and has attracted much subsequent interest from historians. The central evidence of the proceedings are the minutes kept by Colonel Hossbach, known as the Hossbach Memorandum.

Taylor questioned the reliability of this Memorandum. Earlier historians understood from the Hossbach Memorandum that the Hossbach conference had been held to discuss the need for *Lebensraum*. When read alongside Hitler's autobiography *Mein Kampf*, this had been seen as the clearest indication that Hitler had, from an early date, planned a general European war to achieve his goal of more living space for Germans. Taylor challenged this interpretation, making the point that the Memorandum survives as a copy of a copy of the original, which Hossbach had in any event written from memory days after the conference. Taylor wrote of the Memorandum that ' far from being an official record [it] is a very hot potato'.

He claimed that the purpose of the meeting with which the Hossbach Memorandum was concerned had been misunderstood. In Taylor's opinion, the Hossbach conference was called to discuss future re-armament, not war plans. While this could be seen as an indication of Hitler's warlike intentions, Taylor argued that it was in reality a simple matter of internal politics, aimed at out-manoeuvring Schacht, the Minister of Economics, and his financial scruples over the cost of the proposals. In this view, the Memorandum is worthless as evidence of Hitler's war plans. This fits in with Taylor's wider thesis that Hitler, far from having a master-plan in foreign affairs, was an unscrupulous opportunist, who took advantage of circumstances as they arose.

## Taylor's final verdict

Taylor's final verdict on the accidental nature of the outbreak of the war was as follows: 'Hitler may have projected a great war all along; yet it seems from the record that he became involved in war through launching on 29 August a diplomatic manoeuvre which he ought to have launched on 28 August.' The basis of this verdict was that Hitler had intended all along to force the Poles to negotiate over Danzig. Moreover, since the signing of the Nazi–Soviet Pact, he had been putting pressure on Poland's allies, Britain and France, to bring these negotiations about. The pressure had involved winding up tension in the region and making military commitments to his generals. When the timing went wrong (hence Taylor's comment on the dates) and the Poles still declined to negotiate, Hitler was trapped into having to go to war to save face with his generals.

Taylor's analysis never convincingly explained two points:

◆ Why Hitler, in view of the subservient position of the army command following its 1938 re-organisation, could not simply disregard his generals rather than enter an unwanted war.

◆ Why the Nazi–Soviet Pact contained secret clauses which arranged for Poland and the three Baltic Republics to be divided between Germany and the Soviet Union.

Taylor's analysis caused much fury among traditionalist historians. But in his 1964 rebuttal, Taylor was impishly unrepentant. The contrasting interpretations of Hitler's foreign policy and the origins of the Second World War became the basis for perhaps the most famous of the great historiographical debates.

## *The modern debate*

The detail of Taylor's case provided many new insights into international relations in the 1930s. The most telling rebuttal came from those historians who argued that Taylor had failed:

◆ to give sufficient attention to the steady development of Nazi Germany towards a war economy.

◆ to acknowledge how, since 1933, German society under the relentless flow of Nazi propaganda had embraced militarism and gloried in Nazi threats to use force in international matters.

A separate economic argument has been advanced that German foreign policy was by 1938–39 responding to a growing economic crisis in the Third Reich. Re-armament was requiring heavy imports of raw materials and fuel. By 1937, it seemed that continued re-armament would lead to major crises in the balance of payments and the availability of raw materials, rapid inflation and a consequent collapse in German living standards. This line of argument looked at reasons behind Germany's expansionist policy which stretched beyond Hitler's lust for conquest. Speculation on these same lines occupied Hitler in the Hossbach Memorandum, and may well give that document more significance than Taylor was prepared to concede.

R.J. Overy in his book *War and Economy in the Third Reich* (1994) argued that Taylor had been wrong to see the extensive German re-armament of 1938–39 as simply intended to dominate the Czechs and the Poles and ensure German domination of Central Europe. It was the basis for something much more ambitious, namely *Lebensraum* to the east or a challenge to British and United States power in the west. Overy argued that Hitler did not go to war to solve any German economic crisis, or to keep the German people quiet as his re-armament policies led to economic chaos, because this was not necessary. Overy accepted that from as early as 1933, Hitler had aimed to turn Germany into a military superpower by the 1940s. For Hitler, armament and economic policy were servants of foreign policy and not, even in the 1939 crisis, the other way round.

## Compromise

In a classic earlier study, A. Bullock's *Hitler, a Study in Tyranny* (1962) had argued for what became a generally accepted compromise between Taylor and his opponents. According to Bullock, Hitler did hold consistent expansionist aims in his foreign policy, but his great skill was to implement these aims 'with complete opportunism in methods and tactics'. In a later essay in E.M.Robertson's *The Origins of the Second World War* (ed. 1971), Bullock offered the now generally accepted synthesis of Taylor's and earlier views, arguing that in August 1939 Hitler welcomed the prospect of a war with Poland, but had not expected this to involve him in a war with France and Britain. For Bullock, there was no question of a timetable or a blueprint for expansion. Hitler was certainly an opportunist, but one who showed remarkable consistency of purpose in his foreign policy aims and in building up Germany's armed strength. Given this, Bullock concluded that it was impossible to see how war could have been avoided, unless France and Britain had been prepared to abandon all of Europe east of the Rhine to German domination.

W. Carr's *A History of Germany*, first published in 1969 but with three subsequent editions to 1991, also saw Hitler as much more purposeful and intent on specific expansionist objectives than Taylor was earlier prepared to accept:

◆ Taylor, for example, saw Hitler's March 1939 occupation of Prague as 'without design. He acted only when events [in Czechoslovakia] had already destroyed the settlement of Munich'. Carr on the other hand has Hitler 'determined to complete the destruction of Czechoslovakia' from the moment the Munich agreement was signed.

◆ In March 1939, Taylor claims 'The question of Memel appears to have exploded of itself', whereas Carr has Hitler 'compelling' Lithuania to hand back the territory to Germany.

Carr noted that from this point, the *Luftwaffe* (German airforce) started to prepare for war with Britain. He interestingly cited Hitler ordering a five-fold increase in the German airforce, particularly long-range bombers, in October 1938. These plans and the German Z Plan for a large naval battle fleet, Carr argued, arose from Hitler's realisation that after Chamberlain's interference at Munich, he would have to fight Britain, and so France, before 'he could realise his eastern ambitions'. According to Carr, Hitler envisaged such a war taking place in the mid 1940s. Carr agreed with Taylor that the actual timing of *Anschluss* was improvised. But he saw Hitler's subsequent pressure on Czechoslovakia as more purposeful than Taylor allowed, with a deliberate willingness to go to war to obtain his objectives. Carr argued that with regard to Poland in 1939, Hitler 'intended … [to] eliminate what he regarded … as a potential threat in Germany's rear', but agreed that Hitler had assumed that this could be done without involving Germany in war with Britain and France.

## The old view returns

In a recent article in the *Modern History Review* (April 1997), J. Hiden argued that Hitler spent 'much time and energy reflecting on foreign affairs', and by 1933 had developed a coherent strategy for foreign policy. By 1939 his re-armament policy and his expansionist foreign policy had made the outbreak of war inevitable. There is very little of Taylor's thesis of accident and opportunism left standing in this brief but powerful analysis. When the comparatively recent opinions of Carr, Overy and Hiden are considered together, they represent a remarkable shift back to the older view that Hitler had intended both domination and eventually war.

## *Studying historical interpretations of Hitler and the origins of the war in 1939*

**1** First, understand the case of those historians like Churchill and Shirer. Regarding Hitler as evil, they saw him hatching plans to make Germany great and ultimately aiming to dominate Europe. Both Shirer and Churchill's books (see the further reading section) are generally available.

**2** The other side of the debate comes from Taylor. You should dip into his argument at key episodes, using the index and contents pages (see the further reading section).

**3** Then take the major episodes of the 1930s (see the chronology in the Reference Section). Consider how each one can be made to fit the very different interpretations of Hitler's role which you have read.

**4** To carry the debate forward, see the final chapter of this book.

# 7 Conclusions

## Who was responsible for the outbreak of the Second World War in 1939?

**Key points**

◆ Hitler's personal responsibility for German foreign policy
◆ Did Hitler have a master-plan or was he just a skilled opportunist?
◆ The role of other nations in the outbreak of war

## Hitler's personal responsibility for German foreign policy

Hitler's assumption of total power within Germany came swiftly and brutally. With the passing of the Enabling Act in March 1933, he obtained dictatorial powers, and after the political purge of the Night of the Long Knives in 1934, there were no rivals left within his own party.

In his first years in office, Hitler had to be wary of the reactions of the army leaders. The purge of his paramilitary supporters, the SA (*Sturmabteilung*), in the Night of the Long Knives had been partly to allay the army leaders' doubts about the future direction of the Nazi state. After this purge, leading generals like Blomberg had few objections to the general drift of Hitler's foreign and re-armament policy, although they hesitated at his boldness in re-militarising the Rhineland. There was later speculation that if the re-militarisation had failed, then the army might have moved to replace Hitler. After its success, doubts were much more muted, though not immediately stilled. This process was greatly advanced by Hitler's skilful manoeuvres at Munich, which saw the acquisition of the Sudetenland without a shot being fired.

The re-organisation of the army command and the purge of Foreign Office officials in early 1938 had silenced any independent-minded critics. Ribbentrop, the Foreign Minister in the critical years from 1938–45, was simply Hitler's puppet, and executed policy as instructed. The great German capital-ists, content with Hitler's internal economic policies and with Nazi expansion of the army and the armaments industry, did not try to influence the course of foreign policy. From 1934, Hitler's political supporters were his subordinates, and were not colleagues to be consulted. The exception was the Minister of Economics, Schacht. When he opposed expanded spending on armaments, he had to be out-manoeuvred, and was finally dismissed in 1939.

The other possible sources of opposition to Hitler's internal and foreign policies were systematically subordinated to the Nazi state. The press, the trade unions, the universities and the churches were very largely bullied into silence. Until 1939, most German citizens approved of the direction of Hitler's foreign policy, restoring Germany to its rightful place in European politics, and rejoiced in its easy successes. This was only partly because of the effective Nazi use of propaganda. When war came in September 1939, the crowds in Berlin were subdued, but the military triumphs of 1939 and 1940 restored their enthusiasm. It was only remarkably late in the disastrous last months of the war that real disenchantment with the Nazi regime set in.

From 1936 to 1945, Hitler's authority in Germany and over its foreign policy was unchallenged and unimpeded. He alone must be held responsible for its direction and for the methods by which it was pursued.

### Germany's traditional approach to foreign policy

German foreign policy also arose from its history and pre-dated the Nazis. It is increasingly clear that Imperial Germany before 1914 was embarked on expansionist policies in Central Europe which, after the Treaty of Brest–Litovsk with the defeated Soviets in 1918, prompted Hitler's own territorial dreams of *Lebensraum* in the east. Since Germany had been united into one state in 1871, it had always had the potential to dominate Eastern and Central Europe. Versailles had been a terrible humiliation, but it had not broken that potential. Despite its lost lands and the other penalties imposed upon it, Germany remained a great united industrial state. In pursuing his expansionist dreams, Hitler was being loyal to an older German imperial tradition. His foreign policy objectives were not revolutionary, but his methods arguably were.

## Was there a master-plan or was Hitler just a skilful opportunist?

The gulf between those historical views examined in Chapter 6 can be bridged. Recent accounts have tended to argue that Hitler had a more coherent purpose and strategy than A.J.P. Taylor had allowed.

Hitler came to power committed to removing the grievances Germans felt at their unjust treatment at the Treaty of Versailles. This gave his foreign policy a fixed direction which occupied his attention until 1938. He did not however know how he was to achieve his objectives. Taylor was certainly right to see him as seizing tactical opportunities as and when they arose. Examples of this were:

◆ his using the Italian advance across Abyssinia as a convenient moment, with France and Britain distracted and Italy militarily engaged, for his re-militarisation of the Rhineland in 1936.

◆ his arranging the union of Austria and Germany in 1938, despite his original intention of leaving Austria as a separate Nazi puppet state.

◆ his willingness to adapt to Chamberlain's ideas at Munich in 1938.

◆ his exploitation of the disintegration of Czechoslovakia in 1939.

◆ his taking advantage of unrest among the German inhabitants of Memel and Danzig in 1939.

Shirer argued that Hitler had plotted the overthrow of Poland from 1933, with the 1934 Non-Aggression Pact a cynical manoeuvre on the way. This view of

Hitler unscrupulously and deliberately driving Europe to war from the moment he came to power was disputed by Taylor. It seems unlikely that in 1934 Hitler had any clear idea as to how he would eventually resolve the Polish problem, but was simply protecting Germany's eastern frontier whilst pursuing concerns in the west.

It is fair to say that Hitler had definite foreign policy objectives. What is uncertain is whether he had a plan for achieving them. He was very clear that he wished to restore Germany as a full European power. This first involved reversing the most punitive of the terms of the Versailles Treaty. Steps on the way to this included:

◆ denouncing reparations.

◆ starting to re-arm.

◆ re-militarising the Rhineland.

More long-term objectives, with less clear-cut ideas on how they were to be achieved, were:

◆ bringing the Germans in Austria into Germany proper.

◆ bringing the Germans in Czechoslovakia into Germany.

◆ re-adjusting Germany's eastern frontier to re-absorb the Germans in Memel and Danzig.

◆ at least having routes across the Polish Corridor to East Prussia under German control.

In practice, it seems unlikely that these last two objectives were attainable without Hitler going on to seize significant areas of Poland and so cut it off from the sea. Poland was in many ways a turning-point, for Hitler had to commit the might of the German army to battle. When we consider the secret expansionist terms of the Nazi–Soviet Pact, it seems unlikely that this fighting would have stopped short of the total destruction of the Polish state, regardless of French and British intervention. It was no longer a question of simply rectifying the Danzig anomaly. The troops and armour which poured across the Polish frontier and the bombers over Warsaw marked something dramatically bigger. The attack on Poland leads naturally into the question of what Hitler's overall objectives were. From this point, they were increasingly influenced by German military successes, the scale of which could scarcely have been anticipated prior to September 1939.

In 1939, with each objective in turn greater and more speculatively based than its predecessor, Hitler sought:

◆ *Lebensraum* in eastern Europe, with German control of the raw materials and food stocks of European Russia. This was a logical step on from the defeat of Poland, and one which Hitler had repeatedly talked about. The economic arguments for it were compelling. Such a move also fitted Hitler's racist theories about the German master race dominating the lesser races of Europe.

◆ domination of the continent of Europe. Prior to the astonishing German military victories of 1940, Hitler cannot have seen how this could be achieved. A greater Germany, swollen by lands in the east, would have been the dominant European power even without the military conquests, particularly if Hitler's early dreams of Britain and its overseas empire as a natural ally had been achieved.

◆ a challenge for world domination with the United States. It is not at all certain that Hitler saw as far as this, at least until he rashly committed Germany to the Japanese cause in December 1941.

Hitler enjoyed great success with his skilful diplomatic moves, boldness and general bluster prior to 1939. He miscalculated over western reaction to his attack on Poland, but then enjoyed even greater successes, thanks to German military victories. Surely Churchill was right to see Hitler's appetite growing with each success. Certainly his self-confidence, first in his diplomatic ability and then in his military decision-taking, grew dramatically until it brooked no questioning. His appetite for further gains and glory might well have become unbounded by 1941, but they scarcely qualify as a plan. In 1940, there had been no plans in place for an invasion of Britain. German military success had at that point outstripped Hitler's wildest previous ambitions.

# The role of other nations in the outbreak of war

The Second World War came from a particular context. Hitler may well have contributed greatly to its outbreak, but any explanation of why it occurred needs to include both the specific events which led up to it and the responsibility of the other European powers.

## Britain

Britain declared war on Germany on 3 September 1939 in response to the German invasion of Poland two days earlier. This turned a German–Polish war into a general European war. With this single exception, Britain's record was totally defensive though littered with many mistakes, notably:

◆ undermining the fragile Stresa Front by signing the 1935 Anglo-German naval agreement, thus ending the best hope of a collective check on Hitler's dismantling of the Versailles Treaty.

◆ failing in successive crises, particularly with the re-militarisation of the Rhineland, to encourage the French to take a firmer line against German expansion.

◆ underestimating Hitler at Munich in 1938 and failing to support the Czechs at that point, particularly by not involving the Soviet Union in the defence of Czechoslovakia. The contempt Hitler developed for Chamberlain at the time of Munich was the basis of his miscalculation over British help for Poland one year later.

◆ failing, after Munich and after further German expansion in March 1939, to make any serious attempt to reach an understanding with the Soviet Union.

◆ making commitments to Poland in 1939 which encouraged the Poles to refuse concessions to Hitler.

The pact with Poland never convinced Hitler that Britain would go to war to help a country to which it could give no worthwhile support. To do so after the Nazi–Soviet Pact had been signed was quite illogical. In this crisis, the actions and attitudes of Chamberlain, Halifax, the Foreign Secretary from 1938–40, and Henderson, the British ambassador in Berlin, all contributed to Hitler's fatal misapprehension that the British government would never go to war to help Poland.

## France

French distrust of Germany brought about the harsh Versailles Treaty. But in the 1930s, France, which stood to lose most in any future war, lost the will to maintain a firm stand against Hitler's dismantling of the treaty. Internal political weaknesses made French foreign policy ineffective. Notably:

◆ it entered into commitments to smaller states in Central Europe, particularly Czechoslovakia, but never built up the military forces needed to meet these commitments. As a result, it failed to honour its commitments to Czechoslovakia in 1938.

◆ it had adopted a defensive strategy even before Hitler came to power, based on defending France behind the Maginot Line. Even the logic of this was not followed through, for in order not to alarm Belgium, the Line was not extended along the Franco-Belgian frontier.

◆ France, like Britain, acted far too slowly in seeking agreements with the Soviet Union to check Germany, though the greater reluctance lay with Britain.

In September 1939, France declared war on Germany a few hours after Britain. The delay was apparently caused by the French generals wishing to complete the mobilisation of their forces without the threat of a German air attack, rather than through any intention of further negotiation with Germany. In the final week of peace, French diplomacy seemed to be totally paralysed. They communicated neither with the Poles nor the British, drifting into war with no military plans for how that war was to be fought or the Poles to be helped.

## The League of Nations

The League had failed to help China against Japanese aggression in 1931. More seriously, it had then failed to help Abyssinia against Italian aggression in 1935–36. This had severely damaged its credibility. Too many states were no longer members, or had never been members in the first place. It had no military forces to command, and only an ineffective means of enforcing its wishes by using sanctions. The League in the 1930s came to mean only Britain and France, who increasingly pursued their own national interests by direct diplomacy, bypassing the League all together. By 1937 the League was, in W. Carr's words, 'a completely broken reed'.

## The Soviet Union

Under Stalin, the Soviet Union was inward-looking, and often ostracised by the other European powers. The effect of the 1930s purges on its military strength is difficult to gauge, for after performing badly in the 1940 war against Finland, the Red Army then proved a far tougher opponent than the German generals had expected, even in the opening months of their 1941 invasion of Russia. Diplomatically:

◆ in 1938 it was denied a role at Munich. Stalin assumed from this, and from the tardy way in which the Western Powers opened possible defence discussions with the Soviet Union in 1939, that Soviet interests were best served by a deal with Germany.

◆ the Nazi–Soviet Pact of 23 August 1939 opened the way for the German attack on Poland. Its secret clauses, dividing Poland and the Baltic Republics, have been portrayed as totally cynical, though the lands involved had largely formed part of Russia until the First World War. It is arguable that a 1939 Soviet–Western pact would not have saved Poland from dismemberment, for the Poles were as hostile to the Soviets as to the Germans. Stalin might well have been right in his suspicion that Britain and France would have been happy to see 'their' war fought on the eastern front by the Russians.

## Italy

Fascist Italy:

◆ exposed the sham of security under the umbrella of the League of Nations when it invaded Abyssinia in 1935.

◆ helped to wreck the Stresa Front, which had been the one attempt at a united response to Hitler's adventurism.

◆ further undermined any hope of a collective European response to German expansionism by moving into alliance with Germany. In particular, the growing German–Italian links made the French unwilling to take risks in their foreign policy.

◆ helped to polarise European politics by assisting the right-wing in the Spanish Civil War, thus drawing the fascist powers together.

Mussolini's support was needed by Germany at the time of A*nschluss*. But after that, he became increasingly irrelevant to Hitler's plans. He was the intermediary who, at Chamberlain's request, arranged the final Munich meeting. There he posed, for the last time, as one of the great European leaders. In 1939, his warning that Italy was unable to enter a European war because of military deficiencies did not deter Hitler in his pressure on Poland.

## Poland

Trapped between potential enemies to east and west, Poland's right-wing government had little room to manoeuvre in the 1930s. At the end of August 1939, it was clear that Poland was to be the victim of a German invasion. To some extent, the situation on Germany's eastern frontier had been brought about by Polish mistakes and intransigence:

◆ The pact signed with Nazi Germany in 1934 gave no real security (but arguably neither did the 1925 pact with France or the 1939 pact with Britain).

◆ Adding to Czechoslovakia's problems by raising territorial demands at Munich was short-sighted, in view of Germany's evident expansionism.

◆ The Polish refusal, despite French and British pressure, to consider admitting Soviet troops into the country to assist in its defence made protecting Poland from German attack very difficult. This was the rock on which any hope of an alliance between Britain, France and the Soviet Union eventually foundered.

◆ The German case for new arrangements for Danzig and for access across the Polish Corridor was arguably stronger than its demands for the Sudetenland. This was recognised by Britain and France. The Poles however were determined not to negotiate, and were mistakenly strengthened in that resolve by the new British alliance. Unlike the Czechs, they were immune to French and British pressure. For this reason alone, a Munich-style compromise over German demands was not possible.

The Nazi–Soviet Pact sealed Poland's fate. It is unlikely that negotiating with Germany would have given the Poles anything other than more time to prepare for war. By 1939, Hitler had plans for Polish territory that involved more than just concessions over Danzig and the Polish Corridor.

## Japan

The opening of the war in Europe was of marginal interest to Japan:

◆ Its ambitions in the Pacific, particularly with regard to China, were a complication in the 1930s for the United States government, which might otherwise have taken a closer interest in events in Europe.

◆ The unpunished 1931 Japanese aggression against Manchuria gravely damaged the credibility of the League of Nations. To this extent Japan helped first Italy and then Germany defy the League without retribution.

Japan's closer relations with Germany and Italy emboldened Hitler but did not otherwise directly impinge on developments in Europe prior to 1939.

## The United States

The United States never totally isolated itself from European affairs in the 1920s, but a new detachment crept in during the early 1930s as the Roosevelt government struggled to overcome the economic consequences of the Great Depression. Britain's attempts to draw the US into taking an interest in the crises of the late 1930s ran up against isolationist opinion in America and the US government's concerns with Japan. This in turn undermined the best hope that Britain might have made a stand against Hitler prior to 1939.

# How far was Hitler responsible for the Second World War?

The devastation of the Second World War and the racist horrors associated with Nazism inevitably coloured much of the early historical analysis of the period from 1933 to 1945. Taylor insisted that moral judgement was not the province of the historian. It was he who first sought to separate analysis of Hitler's foreign policy from the repugnance at the consequences in terms of human suffering which Nazi policies brought about.

Hitler:

◆ was certainly and increasingly in control of German foreign policy, with few if any restraints in the years 1933–45.

◆ personally contributed greatly to the expansionist national feeling that dominated Nazi German thought on international affairs.

◆ deliberately adopted an aggressive style in his conduct of foreign policy in order to cow opponents.

◆ encouraged successive crises in neighbouring countries and worked to exploit these for Germany's benefit.

◆ grew more and more self-confident and ambitious, increasingly willing to gamble in foreign policy matters.

◆ eventually, in August 1939, either miscalculated seriously about the determination of the Poles and the willingness of Britain and France to support them to the level of war or, less likely, was willing to fight a war on two fronts in order to achieve his objectives against Poland.

◆ may well have realised that he would not be allowed *Lebensraum* in Eastern Europe or domination of the continent without eventually having to fight Britain. Yet in his 1939 Z Plan for an expanded battle fleet and in building long-range bombers, he did not shirk from this prospect.

Despite Taylor, many historians have continued to point to Hitler's ambitions, particularly his stress on the need for *Lebensraum* and his desire for European dominance. They have argued that he was very largely responsible for the tension, the bad faith, the escalating crises that eventually forced Britain and France to back Poland or accept Germany's domination of Central and Eastern Europe and its heavy presence in the West. On these grounds Hitler, planner or opportunist, was almost entirely responsible for the general European war which began in September 1939.

On balance, the argument over how far Hitler had a master-plan for German expansion or simply seized opportunities has gone the way of Taylor, who took the second view. Arguably however, Hitler did have long-term objectives which he used every opportunity to achieve. His appetite grew with his successes, and by August 1939 those successes had come dangerously close to upsetting the political balance in Europe. This, rather than his bullying of Poland or the merits of his claim over Danzig, brought Britain and France to war.

## Studying the causes of the Second World War

**1** In revising this topic for A level and similar examinations, you will not need more knowledge and more ideas than are offered in this book and backed up by one good recent textbook on European history of the period, although further reading will broaden your understanding. Consult the suggestions in the bibliography.

**2** You will need to prepare yourself for answering questions at essay length. Your ideas on the main issues must be clearly thought out so that they are easily available during an examination. Do not prepare ready-made and learned answers, for an unusually worded question will catch you out. Know the subject matter and the theories about it so well that you can confidently adapt them to any form of question. Most of the themes for this topic are obvious from what you have already read.

**3** Be ready to write at essay length on titles based on the following:
- Hitler was a supreme opportunist not a master-planner.
- The Second World War broke out by accident (or miscalculation) rather than by design.
- Nazi foreign policy arose from the militarist, totalitarian nature of the Nazi state.
- British and French policy from 1933–39 contributed largely to the outbreak of war.
- The policy of appeasement was the only sensible one for the British and the French governments to follow.
- There was much to be said in favour of the actions of the British and French governments at Munich.
- The signing of the Nazi–Soviet Pact made a general European war inevitable.
- Why was there peace in September 1938 but war in September 1939?

The same historical knowledge underpins several of these questions. The best way of revising this complex topic will be to practise your response to the issues raised in these titles rather than memorising historical facts about the 1930s. Remember the titles are deliberately controversial in order to encourage you to think about the issues they raise. Be prepared to challenge the assumptions behind the questions.

# *Chronology 1925–41*

**1925**
◆ The Locarno Agreements confirmed Germany's western frontiers and brought Germany fully back into European politics.

**1926**
◆ Germany joined the League of Nations.

**1928**
◆ Germany signed the Kellogg-Briand Pact outlawing war.

**1929**
◆ Wall Street Crash led to world-wide economic depression.

**1933 January**
◆ Hitler became Chancellor (Prime Minister) of Germany.

**1933 October**
◆ Germany walked out of the international disarmament talks.
◆ Germany withdrew from the League of Nations.

**1934 January**
◆ German-Polish Non-Aggression Pact.

**1934 July**
◆ Attempted take-over of the state by Austrian Nazis thwarted by the Austrian Government and Mussolini.

**1935 January**
◆ Plebiscite in the Saarland produced an overwhelming vote to rejoin Germany.
◆ Germans introduced military conscription and openly started to build an airforce.

**1935 April**
◆ Britain, France and Italy proposed to form the Stresa Front against future German aggression.

**1935 June**
◆ Anglo-German naval agreement signed.

**1935 October**
◆ Italy invaded Abyssinia.
◆ Collapse of the Stresa Front.

**1936**
◆ German support for the Italian attack on Abyssinia.
◆ Re-militarisation of the Rhineland.

**1936 October**
◆ Hitler and Mussolini created the Berlin–Rome Axis.

**1936 November**
◆ Germany and Japan signed the Anti-Comintern Pact (Italy signed 1937).
◆ Italy and Germany provided military aid to Franco in the Spanish Civil War.

**1938 March**
◆ German annexation of Austria (*Anschluss*).

**1938 September**
◆ The Munich Agreement on the handing over of the Sudetenland to Germany by Czechoslovakia.

**1939 March**
◆ German take-over of much of the rest of Czechoslovakia.
◆ Slovakia became a German puppet state.
◆ German annexed Memel, a free city supervised by the League of Nations.

**1939 May**
◆ Pact of Steel proclaimed by Hitler and Mussolini.

**1939 August 23**
◆ Nazi-Soviet Non-Aggression Pact signed.

**1939 September 1**
◆ German invasion of Poland.

**1939 September 3**
◆ Britain and France declared war on Germany.

**1939 September**
◆ Poland overrun by German and Soviet armies.

**1940**
◆ Sweeping German victories in Western Europe left Germany in control from the North Cape of Norway to the Pyrenees.

**1941 June**
◆ Germany attacked the Soviet Union.

**1941 December**
◆ Following the outbreak of war between the USA and Japan, Hitler declared war on the USA.

# Further reading

There is a detailed history of Nazi Germany in W.L. Shirer's *Rise and Fall of the Third Reich* (1960), which presents a purposeful Hitler bent on European domination. The traditional view of 1930s international affairs, with Hitler as the ambitious and ruthless villain, is vividly presented in the first half of W.S. Churchill's *The Second World War: Volume 1 The Gathering Storm* (1948). A. Bullock's *Hitler, a Study in Tyranny* (1962) is another classic work, but one which attempts to incorporate revisionist ideas on Hitler as an opportunist rather than just a meticulous planner. All three of these works are widely available in libraries, but the student with examinations in mind will need to dip into them selectively.

The important revisionist work by A.J.P. Taylor, *The Origins of the Second World War* (1961), is best approached through the paperback edition of 1964, which includes Taylor's 'second thoughts' on the controversy aroused by his book. This work can also be found in most libraries. It too should be used selectively, and probably only after a student has gained an outline knowledge of the sequence of events in the 1930s. Both the original book and the 'second thoughts' are deliberately controversial. They raised two important possibilities: that Hitler did not have a master-plan but was a remarkable improviser, and that the Second World War owed as much to accident as to design. Not everyone was totally convinced.

E. Wiskemann, in *Europe of the Dictators* (1966), still saw Hitler's *Mein Kampf* as a systematic plan for national and racial expansion. W. Carr's *A History of Germany 1815–1985* (4th edition 1991) has two valuable chapters on Nazi Germany which present an account of a purposeful Hitler embarked on a systematic attempt to dominate Europe. Chapter 6 of R.J. Overy's *War and Economy in the Third Reich* (1994), which takes a similar line to Carr on Hitler's war plans and the German economy, would reward any ambitious A level student. K. Robbins' Historical Association pamphlet, *Appeasement* (1988), has one chapter, 'Appeasement in Action', which provides a British focus on European events in the 1930s.

For the busy student, articles in periodicals and in collections of essays, especially recent ones, are particularly useful for quickly acquiring ideas. P. Hayes has edited *Themes in Modern European History* (1992) in which P. Bell has a twelve-page essay entitled 'Hitler's War? The origins of the Second World War', which any A level student would benefit greatly from reading. E.M. Robertson (Ed.) *The Origins of the Second World War* (1971) and G. Martel (Ed.) *The Origins of the Second World War Reconsidered* (1986) are other important essay collections. R.J. Overy's *The Origins of the Second World War* (1987) includes a collection of contemporary documents and commentary. *The Modern History Review*, which focuses many of its articles on A level students, regularly features international affairs in the 1930s, as in Volume 8, issue 4 (April 1997), which contains J. Hiden's article, 'Hitler's Foreign Policy'.

# Biographical information

**Beck**, Josef: Polish Foreign Minister who in 1934 signed the Non-Aggression Pact with Hitler and in August 1939 signed the military alliance with Britain. He had earlier refused to bow to French and British pressure to agree that Soviet forces could move into Poland to defend it in any war with Germany.

**Benes**, Eduard: President of Czechoslovakia 1935–38. He resigned in protest at the Munich Agreement requiring the handing over of the Sudetenland to Germany.

**Chamberlain**, Neville: British Prime Minister 1937–40. He was chief promoter of the policy of appeasing Hitler, most notoriously in 1938 at Munich. When, in 1940, the war began to go badly he was forced to resign.

**Churchill**, Winston: British Prime Minister 1940–1945. Out of office in the 1930s his was the main voice crying for Britain to stand up to Hitler and for British re-armament to be speeded up.

**Daladier**, Edouard: French Prime Minister 1938–40. He supported appeasement and signed the Munich Agreement with Hitler but led France into war in 1939.

**Dolfuss**, Englebert: Chancellor of the Austrian Republic 1932–34. His assassination, while attempting to curb the Austrian Nazis, led to Hitler's ill-thought-out 1934 attempt to bring pressure on Austria to unite with Germany.

**Eden**, Anthony: British Foreign Secretary 1935–38, when he resigned because the government declined to put effective pressure on Italy over its invasion of Abyssinia. He was again Foreign Secretary under Churchill 1940–45.

**Goebbels**, Josef: leading Nazi. An effective rabble-rousing orator, he was in charge of German propaganda 1933–45 and was, during the war, given widespread powers within Germany.

**Goering**, Hermann: He built up the German airforce and received great acclaim in 1939–40 at the time of Germany's spectacular victories. In 1937 he had been appointed Foreign Minister and later Hitler's deputy. He was subservient to Hitler over all foreign policy issues and lost credibility when the war turned against Germany.

**Henlein**, Konrad: Nazi leader of the Sudeten Germans. He provoked the disorder which in 1938 allowed Hitler to put pressure on the Czechs prior to Munich.

**Hitler**, Adolf: appointed Chancellor of Germany in 1933, he immediately took dictatorial powers which he retained until 1945. Took the title of *Führer* (leader) and became Head of State in 1934.

**Hossbach**, Colonel Friedrich: writer of the Hossbach Memorandum of a meeting in 1937 addressed by Hitler. Its status and interpretation later became central to the argument among historians about Hitler's intentions in foreign policy.

**Mussolini**, Benito: fascist leader of Italy from 1922. After the collapse of the Stresa Front he moved into closer but increasingly subservient relations with Hitler. In 1938 he arranged the third (final) Munich meeting. In 1939 he had to admit that Italy was not prepared for war.

**Ribbentrop**, Joachim: leading Nazi and a close friend of Hitler. German ambassador to Britain 1936–38 and Foreign Minister 1938–45. He signed the Nazi–Soviet Pact of August 1939 on behalf of Germany.

**Roosevelt**, Franklin: President of the United States 1933–45. In the 1930s, though concerned with international developments in Europe and Asia, his internal commitments and public opinion made him limit the United States role.

**Schacht**, Hjalmar: able German Minister of Economics 1934–39, when he was forced to resign for questioning increased arms expenditure plans.

**Schuschnigg**, Kurt von: Chancellor of Austria 1934–38. He was unable to prevent the Nazi take-over and subsequent *Anschluss* with Germany.

**Seyss-Inquart**, Arthur: Austrian Nazi leader whose scheming brought about the 1938 German invasion of Austria and immediate *Anschluss* with Germany.

**Stresemann**, Gustav: Foreign Minister of Weimar Germany 1924–29. He negotiated better relations with the Western Powers, as at Locarno, but never accepted the eastern frontiers imposed on Germany at Versailles, though accepting that their revision must come from peaceful negotiations.

## German military expenditure (in millions of marks)

| | |
|---|---|
| 1933–34 | 750 |
| 1934–35 | 4,093 |
| 1935–36 | 5,492 |
| 1936–37 | 10,271 |
| 1937–38 | 10,963 |
| 1938–39 | 17,247 |

(R.J. Overy, *War and Economy in the Third Reich*)